DATE DUE

COMPLICATIONS

GARRETT CAPLES
COMPLICATIONS

Meritage Press

ISBN-13: 978-0-9794119-1-5
ISBN-10: 0-9794119-1-2

Meritage Press
256 North Fork Crystal Springs Rd.
St. Helena, California 94574
www.meritagepress.com
MeritagePress@aol.com

Design and composition by Quemadura
Printed on acid-free, recycled paper

Noo soul a-steppèn light like her—
An' nwone o' comely height like her

WILLIAM BARNES

my head is on fire but my feet are in water
a stranger where i've always been
in love with the last long distance apartment
between here and eventual death

my soul is frozen cause my teeth are golden
my eyes are coca-cola red
my balls have developed a mind of their own
consider me self-unemployed

someday the earth will roll through my bones
when i have no use for them
if you drink from my skull please polish the bowl
so you can't taste my memories

CONTENTS

ALL CHEMICAL
Symbolist Poems

POEM WHICH BRIEFLY INTERSECTS WITH ''OLD FATHER WILLIAM''

I was really depressed when my body went to hell. Satan was dressed in wine-dark trousers—imperiously slim, natch—and holding one of those skinny wand microphones like Gene Rayburn on *Match Game*. I was in purple tights, Henry the Eighth-style. I looked like a frog on his hindlegs. "You are old," said the Youth, "as I mentioned before, and a fuck-load uncannily so. Your pin-up days are gone." I tried to fight life's alchemical book, its sketch of the Duchess and the babe whose peppery tears end in a feline smile or porcine corpse, but Christ, by the second round, I'd've gladly given up, if it'd been say, a bar fight, but this was for money, and Sugar Ray's making barf out of me on the mat. My belly floated like butterflies when he shot his blank. Satan yawned and prepared his nails, and hell's celebrities roasted me in my sullen rotunda, not the standard kettle, but one whose figure's given ground without notice in every single direction.

ALL CHEMICAL

for Brian Lucas

admiration of the singular
from the stairs of the same:
a blind flower
in sand waves
its wings veined
and therefore close
around my tale
of plastic flowers
seen through watery media
the umbrella closed
its compass rose
the scissors watch
has come to pass
and I hope my carriage
doesn't slip
on all this
gorgeous
polish

∎

painted yellow alabaster
throws her glow
across the acoustic couch

and I have never known her
to be wrong or wrung
from the hands of the ladder
she holds

shall I be pink
like a dish of soap
and offer you my shell

she wonders
am I strapped in
do I brush the pole
at her barbershop

with my wounded shoulder
is the busstop shelter
enough

for this brief harmonica
this wednesday resignation
or am I stripped
down

a knobby thing she'll pass
and flush to her plunging
throat

o cross-kneed
and painted
alabaster
apologies

I twist
like a handkerchief
caught on a line

on soft and unlikely wings

•

here below mismatched rafters
the homespun aether

floats

like the smell
of a room

that's been on fire

my body should not be
a tapestry

but somehow always is

I'm a red girl
I don't remember

being wool

to the balls
of my feet

in a daze

I light eyes
on naked scenes

around the world

but close
on only one

in an empty

town no one
knits

my brow

.

the buildings repeat open stories:
two dogs drink the same bowl

one's cradle is strung with wire
one's tale is organically wrapped

but chopped. Or is he appealing
to a mirror? The buildings repeat

like broken objects. The pictures of cocks
make an appearance but vanish

soon after
a week of sullen obedience

or a brief bit
of shit with my love

says Sheik
I go down with the Arabs

under the lure
of the defiant English girl

you're no physician of cunt
says she

the appearance of broken objects
repeats some agony

until it becomes a road
two dogs can walk across

eventide: the sun throws shadows
on undulating dunes

the shot of the stones
around our neck

flatters us
into thinking

it's morning
and here we've been

sent out sleepyeyed
by an automatic

teller of tales
in search of happy endings

■

violets down my hair

knees bent
and back
packed

dimple as cunt
        of chin

wood tights
can't control
my clatter

though
birds
refrain

from singing

my familiar
is stranger
to me

attached
by happenstance

yet you think
to come
from womb
with key

you do own
nothing of me

in no sense
could

      cold
innocence

keep me
from singing

the birds refrain

o vice lend
a voice to
the vacant land

its endless book

you can't
put down

inviolate
          stares

          ∎

eyedew
becomes
my cheek

my cock
becomes
une fleur

clouds
become
nuance

montage
becomes
my tag

for the
country
within

my walls
I'll
imagine

my rage
becoming
mirage

a rapist
become
therapist

says
when
drunk

the hat
becomes
a habit

that priests
persist in
living in

the cape
becomes
covered

in ice
for who can
stomach it

pregnancy
becomes
him

■

table
houses secrets
under surfaces

rings pen turns
yet corner wheels
to film burns

lights wax
and hides tan

places pine
for visits

but only mothers come
to mouth

face pins on
pictures
flies peel off
to circle paint

covers crack
with wounds

lace fingers and
clasp hands until
pet leaves

skin smiles love
worms a
           round

           ∎

talk
leaks
gossips
go sip

conduct
s fluid
in wood

aisle
connect
either
with
ether .

whether
you will
or wont
want

string
lights
below
bows

shade
pulls
aside

with hand
kerchief
wings

birds
bark

in the
open

brown
mouth
of sky

with a
single
yellow
tongue

it has
a period
stain

SYNTH

for Jeff Clark

sonic nipple
can you feel sound
those golden pears
whose ethos sprang
in unison

a hardon repairs
to the garden
i tried poetry
to open

hoping
i'd be like
dig

all dolled in
spare diapers
& eye perfume

behold a pink
pause in
performance

as sometimes occurs
a unit of unlit
consciousness
hits on the bassnote
below

scubadivers &
troubadours
are tortured by
the bends

in the flow & flower
of siren desire

swallow lysol
and rinse

the vulture
is a prophet
of undigested
architecture

& inasmuch
as much in
the century
that shit me
out passed

as manic
possession

i'd be like
fuck it

inlaws outlaws
leave me alone
drilling for holes
around nebulous
benthos

soft sofa sobs
don't bother me

thumb tuba
you should
mouth
administers
moist thermostat

sue me
you blue
hortensias

you don't look
too good

you find
yourself
addressing
yourself

as you
as you

gauge your
range of anger

angel of
kind dink
legenda!
love evolves
either organ

laugh to hear
& face to see

got there
got ether
together

earth
mars
venus

venue
rams
heart

& arms
against another
in the absence
of bugs & particulars

blood coils
& recoils
being on
a binge

begin
ning some
thing

til urged
by potent herbs
you leave
the plain

SILENCE LICENSE

prick
crypt

stun
nuts

prod
drop

proud
drips

loose
school

part
trap

tarp
trip

liar
rail

pink
puck

peed
deep

pulp
plop

pap
pap

piss
sip

soda
odor

onion
noise

CHANSON DE GOOGOO

for Michael Palmer

lucid cloud
i owe you
one

my letters days
are numbered

woven below
an amorous
elbow

and refuse to
hawk gutterballs

in refuge
from remorse
the empire

—might i speak
empirically—

empowers them
to burn until
empty only

crowning dismal
spectacle

the grownups
are kidding
themselves

entire shelves
face ignominious

retirement
my buyer says
sell theory now

experience has
its price

and is more
expensive
this year

despite french
intentions

the quick brown
fox jumped over
the lazy fucks

scooby has sold
his lagoon

i have
to behave
like the

boneless
boy

of the assiniboine
indian lesbian
legend

else my kingdom for
portuguese modernism

call me plankwalk
anklepants or tiptoe
joe, p. wheaties

or glassbottom beau
from orono

i needa nodoz
from your prose
but you pose

in those robes
like rousseau

to shoe hoes
to show whos
the boss. i

dont floss
my dents

with tridents
my gents
if im bent

i might vent
sarongs in my songs

but i wont
gob a glob
on a blog

gobble
boggle

or gargle
dried goobers
in gargoyle yard

when art
—the rat

—returns from
the theatre
wounded

or threat
ens to

or grunts
and tugs
at the guts

strung
over

dim ulcers
bored into
dulcimers

my sleep
will be

light
and my
teeth

will de
light

when im
elected
dracula

when i hafta
sup on pus

on purpose
at zun zet
to keep my

opus
zupple

picture my
punctures my
supercunt my

percussive
overtures

my gold dome
rocks as like
to fall

from its
green pillow

low lip
ped cup
returns

to suture
the future

aunty em
sends me
centimes

for old
times spent

sauntering
underground
aimlessly

she believes
its currency

the wolf in her
flowers follows
her howling

down to
the sea

with the kind
of precision
nostril

a good dog
would use

to sniff
drugs
out

instead
she seeks

in tongues
some self
consol

ing art
ifice

el euro
es numbero
uno

dans les
etats unis

parce que
chewbacca
is proper

dirty tea
lucid ditty

holy
holy
holy shit

oil
that is

to quote
the beverly
hillbillies

bad references
tho thankfully

poetrys
not a
job

its a set
of dentures

wobbling
in the lobby
of a library

awaiting
gums

dumb
enough
to swallow

delicious
abundance

file
under
life

or
death

DUB SONG OF PRUFROCK SHAKUR

for Lamantia
and secretly for Creeley

now more than ever
no more than ever

poetry enters
the naked
phase

out of shape
and short
on ends

my phone calls
your camera

to sell you
the news

parachutes for
fashion shoots

the landed gentry
landed gently
on the

far shore
for show

fog lifts
from chalk
cliffs

and shifting
light plays
in every
key

truth decays
in the breath
of a bottle

i nose
for noise

like a perch
flapping

in a peach
passage

fuck
sound

hello

i'm on a
date off
grapes

in a pink
mercedes

from the early
eighties

with a pair
of ladies

from the
republic
of haiti

and they
oughta hate me

but they
masturbate me

and serve
cunt to me

while my
country

is fucking
theirs

a mack ho
economic
plan

very
slavery
amerikkka

lord save us from
international
terror

tell allah
to chill

or go
to hell

no one to
look up to

who the
fuck is
you to

deliver
the heart
of its kidney

expensive
cauldrons

whose
crystals
still glisten

drag on
crystal
dragon

crystal
fish

i'm sorry
you died
at a

time
like
this

last
night

a vision
of your
flying
eyes

be good to
her they
said or

she will
kill you

upside
down dog
choking on
karma sutra

rust mark
melting fire
hydrant into

clone camel
race amid
pyramids

hallucinosis

put the
school
in the
book

fuck all
y'all

you know
who i'm
talkin
g to

A YOUNG GIRL RECALLS MEET-ING ERICH VON STROHEIM

for Barbara Guest

barbara tell it on guitar
this tale of wunderbar

what i remember is
chocolate liqueurs

cordials dressed
as little bottles

a man obsessed
with politesse

offering them with a bow
the heel of an absurd shoe

clicking marvellously
like pool balls, like something

right out of *Confetti Trees*
my girlfriend was dating his son

and i tagged along
—the "third" as we used to say—

to make sure no one got hurt
it was more than the word

"modernism" conveys
now that it's gone

madame von stroheim
was decorous, the son

well-behaved if slightly stiff
when who should rush in

but erich himself
followed by an enormous trunk

the cabby was very unhappy about
carrying in. (Editor's Note:

the luggage suggests
his sudden return

from a touring troupe
of *Arsenic and Old Lace*

en route to play rommel
in *Five Graves to Cairo*

if this is los angeles
1943) it touches me

to think of his poverty
when i remember the size of the tip

—not once did this director permit
his work to be finished on schedule—

and no one met him at the station
because we weren't expecting him

but there he was, very germanically
welcoming us to a house

he hadn't lived in in years
it was an act but sincere

he loved his son
he was married to valerie

though he lived in france with denise
since *Grand Illusion*. (Only by chance

was he in america making
I Was An Adventuress for zanuck

when paris fell —Ed.) sad
with a different kind of sad

a love poem love
gone modernist

he produced
from his trunk

the exquisite box
uncovered its contents

and proffered
chocolate bottles

brilliantly foiled
containing fluid

a succulent row
with the air of one

who bestows his most
precious gift

which it
was

THE ROGUE HAGUE

for Andrew Joron

Incorporating Three Poems for Anna, Rock Poems, and Elegies

Capitalism in a sense is an unreserved surrender to things, heedless of the consequences and seeing nothing beyond them. For common capitalism, things (products and production) are not, as for the Puritans, what is becoming and wants to become; if things are within it, if it itself is the thing, this is in the way that Satan inhabits the soul of someone possessed, unbeknown to him, or that the possessed, without knowing it, is Satan himself.

GEORGES BATAILLE, *The Accursed Share*

the trapdoor is closed; am finite again, but a moment ago—levitation!
purple lights the bluewater bridge turned on the oil-
black river st clair became fuel for the nightfishers there
it was the dream of a memory or the memory of a dream
that dumped me below a window, watching a woman change
into a man. she entered his dairy log: *at first all the world was america*
and didn't that suck, he thunk, and strunk his cunk against
an overwrought iron fence. they stood waiting like that photograph
of the bootblack jack and the aristocrat

                                looking away from her window
at a fact well worth recording—Alexander Graham Bell wanted to call
his daughter Photophone. between the forest and the gander
i hand her over to Metacomet. yes i certainly did.
and King Philip sayeth unto me: nature denatured thee
friction alone makes her come therefore i need some more
before you make me wear'um pants. O failed invention!
where'd you get that voice? refusing to come
to a particular point, castration finally made sense.

TURNING ON THE TONGUE

for Barbara Guest

in a joint near
a babbling book

i unconsciously turned
on my tongue

it kept on waking
more asleep

from a taste of
the bud of being

the author employed
various figures

to convey
the idea, like

evergreen
cypresses

form the
appropriate image

of death; this is
compared to

a flower
unexpanded

nice picnic
anyway. no one

carried salt but
we carried bottles

to capture
the atmosphere

and though the raven
lacked communion

with the doubled down
book on the lawn

we finally found
how to fuse horns

watching its
sable pinions

UNTITLED

Imagine a town with no numbers. Did I say *a town*? I more meant *expanse* of unplanned plains, or optional intersections. Fields, some trees. No commerce, of course, no work 'cept for food, and who wants to eat alone? (I picture spontaneous picnics.) *The individual is still accepted, hate* is not unknown, but demand for solitude's grown so rare we lacked concepts for its expression. *She wants to be with herselves*, let's say, or even, *with the trees*. Where? Over there, for we lost track of North and South. The sun doesn't rise so much as light surrounds us until we ascend into night. We killed people, it's true, to adjust their attitude, but could you have lived in their town? A house that was eating itself before it was even home? My bed was in the fireplace. Porcelain cats are cold. Blood seeps under the ballroom floor where the creature bit off its sex. They never found it; the ground swallowed. Now people can lie on the grass and dream. The mountains are anywhere the reclining journey begins. Gorge on its purple pines. Squint at the church of obsidian ribs hidden in its chest. Horses pour from one another. Their skulls branch over the living quarter. The town might appear in a grave rubbing, its sky no void but cataract. Those tears of eros look like diamonds but taste like shit, and they cut the world's oval throat in a delicate squirt of hibiscus. The tiny blots that spatter blossom into little birds.

INSIDE THE COIN

And it was into interiors of all kinds that he was invariably drawn, as if fulfilling the old hermetic-magical invitation, in order to acquire knowledge and power, to go "into the insides of the earth." So, lo, to the extreme delight and wonder of children, Mandrake took off one day for what was to be his longest adventure; he descended into another universe, to another inhabited planet which existed in the sub-atomic spaces within the interior of an American coin! Among childhood friends and acquaintances this series of comic-strip adventures "inside the coin" was the source of endless reveries at every chance turn in the long chain of phantasmagoric events.

PHILIP LAMANTIA, *"Radio Voices"*

The signs advertising the new dollar—this a gold disc with a sexy, over the shoulder shot of Sacagawea—elide the entire motivation of the campaign (get used to it so we can retire the unreliably paper-based Washington head) by employing the very icon they seek to dismiss, collaged in banal circumstances designed to ease our transition into the heretofore undreamt realm of "coin" currency. Clearly our government's unwilling to commit another Susan B.-level disaster, for her pouting pewter profile endeared her to no one, and the persistent assumption of her Sapphism, fanned by her fame as a suffragette and the concurrent invention of the "lesbian money" stamp, has effectively been countered by proof of this pretty native's heterosexual bent, a slumbering child in her backpack, thus motivating her position in both flirtation and stolid American belief in the naturalness of family. But the particular tack of pasting the familiar Washington head into a variety of bourgeois scenarios—this George wears sweaters and carries an umbrella in case it rains—this method of soothing citizen-consumer's nerves as he contemplates the heathen metal, savage like its portrait, the coin that much closer to raw money, like bullion or ore—this strategy of proffered identification with the head of the father of our country suggests, in its desperate insistence, some of the psychological motivations behind America's notorious resistance to monetary change. For money, being the only collective cultural god in American history, uniting all castes and colonists, immigrant through aristocrat, is the image in which we are made; we can't help but take it personally, and regard it with the superstition accorded a tribal fetish. Take, for example, the changes in bills, denominations Lincoln through Franklin. The old small head design will soon seem arcane as red writing on silver certificates, yet at present, the new large off-center heads alienate the surviving 20th Century population, even frighten it in a manner roughly akin to a 19th Century cinema audience fleeing the approach of an on-screen train. Fortunately, in terms of our government's cause, we've absorbed the techniques of cinema to the point of invisibility. Whatever artist designed this campaign might even be credited with a minor inventional variant on previous generic categories, concocting from their table scraps a sort of absurdorealist aesthetic. Though print, the new dollar ads strike me as cinematic precisely due to the nature of this realism. Their brand of absurdism has been seen in at least two prominent recent examples, sufficient to cause stirrings of faint recognition in the shallow pool of collective cultural memory: those *South Park* episodes in which the likes or rather likenesses of Saddam Hussein or David Hasselhoff are photoshopped into the otherwise cartoon universe; and the queer third-person adventures of Mr. Jenkins in *Tanqueray* gin ads, again photographed heads on tiny cartoon bodies. The new dollar ads turn this absurdism inside out, however, by imposing cartoon—or engraving as the case may be—onto photograph, relegating the realistic to the background, where it's at its most insidious. The background of most Hollywood films, allegedly establishing the plausibility of a world in which implausible events will occur, is in fact itself generally established by the convincingness of the protagonist offered us for identification purposes.[1] If we admire the irrepressible spunk of the waitress struggling under

1. This is not the case in meticulous compositions in which directors like Von Stroheim constantly work the background for both subtle psychological and overtly symbolic effects. An example of both at once: Von delights in manipulating Roman Catholic iconography, but only rarely does he draw attention to it. If you pick up on this one of his several tics, you begin to notice he uses it as a pliant formal code—the same object will indicate different things at different times —for commentary on certain scenes. In the scene at *Francois'* in *The Merry Widow* (1925), when John Gilbert suffers the pangs of presumed rejection by Mae Murray, Jesus suffers right there with him, baroquely and bloodily from a crucifix near the window Gilbert stares out of. When he finally turns around, after imagined hours pining at stars, he notices Murray did not storm out bitterly as he'd supposed but is instead crashed out right there on the couch. Sure enough, a painting behind her depicting Christ taken down from the cross testifies to the cessation of his torment. Put baldly it sounds like Christmas ham, I know, but keep in mind Von seldom foregrounds such devices, simply hoping repeating viewers will see and risking the probable odds they won't. In this he is very like a poet.

low pay, a lecherous boss, and irritable customers, we're more in-clined to accept as real a world where her off-work fits are Prada head to heel, and even, in some cases, mistake it for our own. That's where George comes in. The campaign's target group be-ing America's most moneyed—particularly those white, middle or higher-class men who sit at home stressing about money—it takes no risks in its choice of setting (or costume—you needn't find George in dress or dashiki, who cares what they think!). George's apartment comes straight out of some '90s TV myth of Manhattan; most typical bourgeois couldn't even afford it—ma-hogany walls, brick, sharper image lighting—but it serves as a template of aspiration by which you can at least gauge your pad according to how many imaginative degrees it falls short. More to the point: like the "you" the ad implies, this George sits at home similarly concerned about money, but look!—he's not worried. He's happy about the new dollar, perhaps even think-ing *retirement at last!* And if he's all right with it, how can we fail to be? In god we trust, as our god himself, since the 1950s addition of that jingle onto his person, has never failed to remind us.[2]

2. Since this piece was written, the Sacagawea dollar has more or less failed to propagate and is being replaced by presidentially-headed coins (apparently a se-ries, beginning with George, natch). Americans are suspicious of money unsanc-tioned by a president or founding father. Perhaps this is best. Putting a Native American on u.s. currency is a rank hypocrisy, given the approximately 200-year campaign of genocide against Native Americans dating back to our country's colonial era and their continued oppression in reservations that are little more than open-door concentration camps. Perhaps Sacagawea will find a home in the politically-motivated Indian Casinos, which merely provide a service to white people and constitute a contemptible version of atonement.

stars are wet with children dressing
                              cutting loose horse hair
blood arrows stone the sea
from the moon's diamond wounds
eyes fire poison mouths to swallow

at midnight stone lions
accost drunken clowns dressed as priests
the moon's boudoir is a brothel of blood

the stone is a diamond with blood in it
as the children who fire it know

THREE POEMS FOR ANNA

BIANCA AS I FOUND HER

attic of woods, champagne of ideas, swarm to my rim

archer of tongs and anchor of *what?*, glue to the hoof of my mouth

trombone collector and lifetime investor in valves, throw me some
    clothes for emotion

the vague I value I give to you

muppets doing stints for saints, missing tiles from silent scrabble

steps from snap-it-together kits filled with bituminous mud

the stairs that blush and crumble to dust from sudden human heat

that lead us back to the cellar of funk under the frostlight of stars

escape from essence like sulfur and salt

back to the bottom, circular saw, assiduous love

coffee for ruined surfer

this is not music to skate by, some scum skimmed from
    creamsicle wheat

the cleateaten clef that stirs you, that traces signs on the
    shifting surface

of a beach in an hourglass

that I flail to keep abreast of

that falls like a molten compass

sings in perpetual mulch and breath

my object is never to be at rest

not while the carpet is rolling smoke
and the earthquake snakes past loin
and the heart blows its mind on a spine violin
whose neck is downed with fire
this fire I fix as a votive for you
medicine bell, unused noon, transparent throat of the ocean
brick of tremulous pearl
in the brass coat of walking waking I reach beyond the
      promised limit
past slow morguefill and dog logistics
to comb our inner air
in its coal vault wall the diamond flaw unzips like alien coke
we're buried beneath piñatafall
and the maid's stolen my plastic tongue
can I borrow yours, liquid broccoli, barbequed film
triple halfmoon of marrow
your lips break the thread of this chrysalis
to lynchpin my suspect warmth

come walk come walk come walk with me
to the past in tense but present in box

ice cream coffins in russian detroit
a stack of cars in the barn of a church

that's liable to hit you
falling down. i went from

attic fear to dismantling attic
without pause to experience cause for fear

the jerks that accompany waking
aren't always human but they resemble

human parts. remember the camera
you found in her eye, filming itself

over and over in people's reactions to it
talk about genre painting itself

ancient children in lingerie; a pie
consumed; balalaika tire swing

the announcer reminding his listeners
the iraqi oud players did not initiate

this conflict. in mandarin, michigan sounds
like mexico; we just drew a line to straighten

its nose and now it could pass for moscow
today i turn fifty forever

god mopes in his sober robes
he still owes my company money

for snow we made last year

TRUSTING YOU RECEIVED THE CHERRIES ALL RIGHT I AM YOURS

she is an hourglass, a design
a quilted lining

whose fingers clasp
a white-quilled pen

to an open pad
her one hand holds

like red ribbons drawn through tubes
the horizon is pink and blue

the park's in the path to portugal
sam yellow is slung in his boat asleep

a communication from below
mutely roars

her breasts have berries in them
her legs are half-imagined

she weaves dry waves of mountains
where she faces behind

a window blown
in the wall

behind green bars
sewingmachines plant felt

and i am mad to those who hurt her
i bite off their balls
and swallow
without ceremony
roundeyed and queer

and when she's gone
wet foot
falls attached
to no one

still navigating
porpoise death

unmoved since last
year's painting

the sea pig remains
of coleridge dreams

the city rounds
not squares

my eyes are
nude pagodas

buffalo wings
bring tears

sheet flaps
on a line

like a slowly
frying egg

seeping refrains
from screaming

arab death
in the forest of stèle

WRITTEN ON SEPTEMBER 11, 2001

America has reaped what it has sown, and the sorriest thing is, instead of assessing its own responsibility for allowing such a bigoted fool as George Bush to "lead" our nation, it'll probably rally around him. This I refuse to do, and not out of any admiration for an evil so well-coordinated it seems straight out of some bigoted Hollywood film. Thus far, the one historical comparison to the destruction of the World Trade Center and attack on the Pentagon—despite its almost entire irrelevance, given the differences in the type of world and type of execution that separate these incidents—happens to be the very event recently transformed into an epic romance on the smug screens of America, Pearl Harbor. Today's attacks, however, prove that death isn't sexy like an event that occurred some 60 years ago in period costume. It's grisly, and even if I wanted to take pleasure in a comeuppance as ghastly as the crimes our own nation has perpetrated against humanity—you name it, the deaths of millions of Iraqis from our 10-year embargo; the slaughter of Serbia; our economic exploitation of third-world countries to maintain our inflated standard of living; our blithe disregard for the irreversible environmental damage we've caused; our tacit support of Israeli and Turkish efforts at genocide, you name it—even if I wanted to view this "terrorism" as cosmically just, hits on corporations and the industrial military complex, I simply can't; there's no way to calculate how many innocents were killed—or how to decide what even constitutes innocence—and we have to give the major news media credit, it's kept the people of our country uninformed and insulated to such an extraordinary extent, the few true disclosures of our activities abroad that filter through serve as no more than a built-in margin of error. Most Americans have no context for what has just happened, which keeps them primed to accept whatever reaction the administration decides to make, against whomever. Immediately, before there was any shred of evidence on which to base a guess, news reporters promoted an "Arab" interpretation of whodunnit, even as they denounced unspecified rivals who would have you accept pure speculation as truth. To fill airtime, the Nostra-damically-inclined among the press seized on the date—September 11, the same as the signing of the failed Camp David Accords by the U.S., Israel, and Egypt in 1978—as the motivation and proof of Palestinian involvement. (One NY reporter told KPFA that he heard from the police scanner a description of two suspicious-looking Arabs with backpacks leaving the area, as if the perpetrators could still be alive or the planners would want to observe firsthand.) At the moment, however, speculation has hardened into certainty that Bin Laden is the culprit, and Bush's stated eagerness to retaliate not only against the terrorists but any country who would harbor them seems like a threat tailor made to the Saudi Muslim's exile in Afghanistan. Taken as given is the widespread hatred of America by the average Middle Easterner and the question of why is seldom posed. Mightn't our continual fucking over and around with various Middle Eastern peoples have something to do with it? Mightn't George Bush's imbecilic saber-rattling, which has simultaneously alienated the Middle East, Asia, and indeed much of Europe, been an immediate catalyst to the situation? Or being one of only two countries to withdraw from the recent UN conference on racism, held in South Africa, because certain countries wouldn't compromise with our interpretation of the world? Seen this way, today's attack takes on the appearance of a grim, inevitable logic. The Bush Administration is making our country pay for years of cavalier terminology around tragedies we've created or crimes we're about to commit. Mad with the implications of our self-designated status as the world's only superpower, our willingness to withdraw from any treaty that no longer suits us presupposes the rest of the world must and will tolerate our selective obligations. And it doesn't take a political science background to guess such a proposition is not in the rest of the world's interest. While I'm amazed and appalled at today's events, I'm not at all surprised by them, and I'm neither clairvoyant nor brilliant nor even particularly well-informed. But if you even half pay attention to international events, if you learn to read against the news you hear—to see what a news story wants you to think and assess whether you should think it—then the possible motivations of any of several nations become more than apparent. Our complacency is largely invisible to us, and when it occasionally becomes apparent, it overwhelms us with its torpor. Who doesn't by now know about Nike sweatshops and why hasn't this affected its status as America's number one athletic shoe at all?

We don't want to know. Today's attacks show that we must. The secure feeling that the U.S. mainland is beyond the reach of the conditions of modern warfare has perhaps been permanently breached. This is the chief source of our country's outrage; people without any personal connection to NY, DC, or the victims are frothing because they're suddenly confronted with their own fear of death in a way that just doesn't register watching car bombs and missile destruction in some dusty beige place far from home. If this event provoked any self-reflection on the international practices of the United States, the no doubt 1,000s of victims of today's attacks will not have died utterly in vain. But if it creates the usual solidarity behind a government in crisis—as we never tire of observing in the countries we bomb—what else can follow but greater and greater bloodshed? Our arrogance will be appeased so long as the blood is not ours, the carnage invisible, but the self-satisfied feeling that, no matter what our foreign policy is, we're still safely out of harm's reach, may never return. The United States is only an infantile empire and civilizations of far longer duration have disappeared from the earth; this is our first real taste of potential non-permanence. Our mistake has been the Dorian Gray one of projecting our current image of ourselves infinitely into the future, unsullied by our actions. Our collective outrage, however, can't possibly match our global outrageousness and the most immediately responsible parties to this crime are an arrogant and imperial leadership given free rein by an indifferent and ignorant population.

THE DELICACY OF AMBROSE BIERCE

. . . that prose has its prosody no less exacting than verse.[1]

From the days of his first notoriety as "The Town Crier," a column he wrote from 1868–72 in the *San Francisco News Letter*, Ambrose Bierce has been labeled a bitter misanthrope by detractors and admirers alike, the latter group itself divided into those who condone this as a virtue and those who concede it, magnanimously, as a flaw. To his contemporaries he was known as "Bitter Bierce," and while he would on occasion demur, he didn't go too far out of his way to correct this impression, for it was of inestimable value to him as a writer who cultivated the indignation of railroad magnates, politicians, and a host of less formidable foes, authors of all stripes included. The fact that in 1913 at age 71 Bierce stalked off into Mexico to follow Pancho Villa's army, only to vanish without a trace after a final letter from Chihuahua dated December 26th, has sealed his reputation in a keg of brine, insofar as this peculiar retirement was motivated by a prodigious disgust with the United States. But Bierce was not bitter; that is, the quality to which this unanimous testament bears witness—citing the barbed definitions of *The Devil's Dictionary* and the chronic morbidity of his short stories—is not bit-

1. From "The Matter of Manner," reprinted in M. E. Grenander's edition of *Poems of Ambrose Bierce* (Nebraska, 1995), page 134. Hereafter cited as PAB.

terness but rather one of the most profound examples of black humor to be found in American Literature.

Bierce disappeared on the eve of the First World War, and while the formulation of l'humour noir postdates that conflict, the concept's wide acceptance has followed from its evident applicability to writers of the past. Nineteenth century authors, including Americans like Poe and O. Henry, occupy a good half of André Breton's eventual Anthologie de l'humour noir (1945), and even the most ardent citizen would be obliged to admit the U.S. of the late 1800s afforded abundant material to the black humorist. To my knowledge, Bierce is the only literary figure of note to have fought in the Civil War, on the same battlefields he'd revisit in 1913 en route to Mexico.[2] At the outbreak of hostilities, the 19-year-old immediately enlisted in the Union Army, rising through the ranks to First Lieutenant as he survived some of the war's bloodiest battles. In 1864, he was shot in the head— "which," to invoke his own sardonic understatement, "made a deep impression on him at the time"—and the following year he served in Selma, Alabama as a member of the Treasury Department's occupation force, subject to the typical discomforts inflicted thereon by an armed and resentful local population. Is it any wonder that besides a lifetime of severe headaches resulting

2. Only after this text was first published did I learn of the lesser known but brilliant writer of Poe-like weird tales, Irish-born New Yorker Fitz-James O'Brien (1828-1862). Like Bierce, he enlisted in the Union cause due to abolitionist sympathies, distinguished himself for bravery in battle, and got shot (albeit in the shoulder). Unlike Bierce, O'Brien died of his wound.

from his wound, the war left Bierce with a permanent vocal in-
tolerance of the empty appeal to sentiment in which corpora-
tions and politicians clothe naked greed, a fashion known then,
as now, as patriotism?

That black humor imbues Bierce's war stories—particularly
his depictions of ludicrous attitudes the body may assume on
occasions of sudden, violent death—can hardly be denied. Yet
he often distills his blackest, most refined essence in the more
parlor-like setting of the magazine essay, as a critic of his cul-
ture's jingoistic conceit. Consider his response in 1901 to an un-
named author's inquiry whether Washington or Lincoln was
"the greatest man this country ever produced":

> In my judgment neither of the men mentioned is entitled
> to the distinction. I should say that the greatest American that
> we know about, if not George Sterling, was Edgar Allan Poe. I
> should say that the greatest man is the man capable of doing the
> most exalted, the most lasting, and the most beneficial intellec-
> tual work—and the highest, ripest, richest fruit of the human
> intellect is poetry.... [N]othing that [Washington and Lincoln]
> built will abide. Of the "topless towers" of empire that the one
> assisted to erect, and the other to buttress, not a vestige will re-
> main. But what can efface "The Testimony of the Suns"? Who
> can unwrite "To Helen"? (PAB 148)

To champion Edgar Allan Poe over George Washington for
the title "greatest American" requires a certain amount of ef-
frontery. To propose a comparatively obscure contemporary
poet like George Sterling is to make a supreme gesture of faith,

beyond the orbit of bitterness, even as Bierce's withering summary of U.S. history unfurls his unflagging unbelief. For Bierce is in dead earnest, unruffled by the unlikelihood of anyone's assent, and as a corrective to America's sense of its unique importance and permanence, he offers *The Iliad* and the disappearance of the culture that produced it. "Art and literature," he concludes, "are the only things of permanent interest in this world" (PAB 151), and this profession discloses the luminous point of his negation. For this is not an aestheticist doctrine, but rather the conviction of one who took a long view of history and who, having looked into death's maw yet unaccountably survived, found no small amount of consolation in literature. By no means unconversant in the genteel tradition, Bierce writes of fancy as one intimate, and is without peer among nineteenth century American writers as a critic of poetry. From the immersion of this refined, one might say delicate, sensibility in a culture of extreme violence emerges a black humor of incalculable depth.

ON THE SEPARATION OF
ART AND BILLY COLLINS

goosepimple palace displays
a wooden spoon ruler

asleep with one cartoon
foot on the moon

loads of drool purling
to fool his goons

a pool party mood ensues
among the wool pullers

whose thought balloons
soon mushroom to

the tune of cool billions
the root of all proof

bit the roof loose
with a tattered tooth

to scoop up blood
from the killing floor

food is too bitter
in this cocoon

the gloom of global warming
floods poor new orleans

to make room for whitey
to groove. this afternoon

the scrooge age resumes
its droopy boobs

and tools around
on a crooked broom

cooking a boolean
lasso to noose

my spooked appaloosa
see here magoo

support our troops
is moot on a good

suv. with doomsday
looming on the books

and kangaroo courts
cooping up stooges

in human zoos
the boozy coots

snooze as poodles
jump through hoops

and google boys
to doodle noodles

in the bloopers reel
they goo pantaloons

and poop piles of loot
with economic booms

booty calls are under
stood in the hood

but loopholes
took the bloom off

our national lampoon
look at the door close

ROCK POEMS

i was a teenage gingerale: my bubbles spiraled upward and rippled a puddle of ironing board. i was a pile of bored, all tusk and wart, i saw i was screwed and hammered. the more i tooled around the box, the more i stammered glamorously. amorously it was freaky. my speaking came out of sequins, in pudenda-purple puzzles and penis-verdi cubes. i got used to boobs and tubes, iffy lube, the protuberance of obvious wobble. later on they hired me to make fake swears for real tv, like *bullshuttle!* and *lincoln!* and i'm thinkin i'm hoggin the login on mobbin.com when all along i'm bobbin for shlong in some conglomerate lawnjockey's puptent. this list could go on but it won't thank god and it isn't for want of content. its haunted constant, coz, is was.

MAJOR APPLIANCES FOR LOVERS IN TIME OF WAR BY Q. P. DAHL, MANUFACTURER

a crypt in description pumped something for pumpkin or other. i heard the trumpet dump it: o chunky dumpling, what's eating you? the thin in think nothing is thin. love it seems has triumphed over virtue, my core coercive vice, picture of a future corpse. the tuba pooped a furtive overture: lamplit armpit, certain curtain, curtailed details prevail. cupid piddles around. bird fiddles and diddles. viol threatens to loose a feather full in ether's teeth. even food's in the mood for rude behavior. pears pair, grapes grope, plums lump out for dim sum. a lone banana ramas. i am ousted from dusty study by a whiff of my wife's enamel. i hitch my camel to her post and roast in her upholstery. follow my nose down the bellyphant road to a gold tinted rose with eros. satin eggs and sausage usage. double hearttocks! strike on back! with a name like crane and a neck to match, my love with the arcimbaldos attacks.

A LITTLE WHITE NOISE
FOR LITTLE WHITE BOYS

our rock was entirely gothic. my people were fair and had ky in
their hair; your people were foul and didn't bring towels. other-
wise we got along. my fowls were purple and howled like a hard-
ened case of the nipples. you boiled your owls in powder and
ground them into chowder. we came at each other like egg-
plants; we commenced to get down. my chickens were kickin
and straight outta Dickens, but your owls had trowels and had
read *The Cask of Amontillado*. by the second verse all hell broke
loose. your devils were clever and played heavy metal while mine
were just plain old bastards. they plastered themselves on Lister-
ine and sucked on harmonica. your devils had a sister named
Louise whose love of cheese was known even over the telephone.
my telephone was run by gnomes who wouldn't accept your
trolls. your trolls had gone home, along with your people, who
packed up their phones and their chowdered owls and chartered
a bus outta town. your owls had disemboweled my purple fowls
with their trowels so there wasn't much point in taking them.
my people had gone with the nipples. soon it was just you and
me. we were naked under our clothes. my hose had holes and
your shoes were easily misconstrued as toes. we blew each other's
nose and did voodoo in our underoos. this was the goal of all

rock. then Louise returned with a mixed party of your people and my people and the few remaining devils, who brought their own owls, and, using the trowels to make a brick stove, boiled the dead fowl in owl chowder. we were briefly a community. Louise handed out Listerine. my people got drunk and started to funk while yours were content with rubber cement. your devils wore sweaters and wrote dirty letters that made my gnomes indignant. your trolls responded with a despondent guitar solo entirely inappropriate to the song. who gave them Danelectros? the souls of my chickens rose in protest and my hose was spraying Dickens. your people grew hungry again and it looked like your shoes had been chewed. the world was all old and folded. the harmonica was gone and Louise faded out like someone who never was. the telephone was cold, the coda colder. the end of the song threw its long shadows against us.

ROBOCOP IMAGINES
ACCEPTING OTHER ROLES

robocop was seen at the oakland docks, throwing bolts at himself & shooting into the crowd. robocop emerged in miami, busting heads at the speed of sound. robocop was spotted near the syrian border, handing out body armor to an appreciative combat unit. covered in what appeared to be a brown substance, robocop entered a local museum in search of weapons of mass destruction. on being a famous war hero, robocop said, it was involuntary; i'm robocop. robocop spent his eightieth birthday skydiving in order to encourage activity among senior citizens. ROBOCOP ELECTED GOVERNOR OF CALIFORNIA! the body of robocop was laid to rest today in a crypt on the grounds of the robocop memorial library. robocop denied fresh allegations of wrong-doing in a closed panel session. in a reversal of his previous statement, robocop claimed he only threw away his ribbons, not the medals themselves. all night long robocop dreamt of saint juste. robocop confirmed he was in talks with the bond franchise to direct a remake of *Casino Royale*. robocop was briefly taken into custody yesterday by venice beach police officers responding to a domestic disturbance call; he was released without charge. fulfilling "a lifelong ambition," robocop captivated broadway this season as the artful dodger in a revival of *Oliver!*

a spokesperson for robocop refused to comment on speculation the mechanized crimefighter had married j-lo over the weekend. according to "his reading" of *The Iliad*, robocop informed a crowded lecture hall, achilles and patrocles were just really good friends. in his final film, robocop played a french convict disguised as a priest whose flight to rome is highjacked by hippies epousing the algierian cause. robocop was treated for minor abrasions after his chevy northstar struck a house during an otherwise routine pizza run. on leno robocop admitted he blew off the premiere of *Robocop III* in order to attend a knicks game. in recent testimony before the fcc, robocop called the idea of *wardrobe malfunction* "implausible at best." robocop issued a rare public apology today for savagely beating a reporter who mistook him for data. robocop spent most of the month of august chopping wood on his crawford texas ranch. robocop was recently named *Motor Trend*'s car of the year. this holiday season, why not stun her with a robocop?

MEMOIR OF THE GRADUATE POETICS PROGRAM

I was A's third husband within the department. I'd come to study the poems of B with C, but C wasn't there anymore and I had no intention of fucking D, so I had a lot of time on my hands. Sometimes the other husbands and I would go for walks, but it was cold, and I had little in common with any of them, except E, who was a tennis player, not a poet. (At least E drank!) I started hanging out with F, and we quickly became lovers even though I was already married. But her poetics were going nowhere, so I soon hitched my wagon to G, whose fellowship was the envy of everyone else. But he immediately left me for H, whose father had made it in raisins, and by now I'm like, I gotta get with one of the teachers if I'm ever going to make the big reading! But it was harder than I thought; I introduced me to J but we didn't get along despite some regard for each other's work. I began a flirtation with K, but K made considerably less than J—"just like the real world"—so she couldn't really support me. Finally I settled on L, for, despite the fact no one liked his poems, L had position —meaning he could fuck—and he'd gotten tenure back when you could get it by mail. But M, my advisor, advised me against it, and instead hooked me up with N, who refused to return my calls after the first fuck, so I turned to O for solace, because, let's face it, he'd fuck almost anyone, but he was already in bed with P by the time I got to his apartment. In despair, I called Q in Thailand and he convinced me to join him—"there's plenty to fuck," he said, "and you only write poems when you want to"— but I was waylaid en route to the airport by R, who offered me a teaching assistantship in exchange for sex, so we fucked until the add/drop period ended. That evening I fled in my nightshirt, only to get caught in S's headlights. We'd read together once a long time ago, so she drove me to her house and gave me some clothes, but wouldn't let me stay the night. I called T to come pick me up and, though he said he usually didn't get down like this, since I was in a skirt he'd fuck me for one night and pretend to not know. The next morning, I was late for coffee with U, who I found at the café busily preparing a list of everyone he'd fucked in the program. I scanned its columns for ideas. Finally I settled on V because he was seated at the next table, but all V wanted was a handjob in the car while he drove to class, after which I was on my own again. W's seminar was about to begin, but W wasn't a poet, so fucking him was out of the question. X's workshop was about to let out, but chances of hooking up were slim. Finally I saw Y heading across campus, but when I caught up to her, all she would offer was a golden shower under the footbridge. I couldn't turn it down. By now my appearance was beginning to attract attention, and I'd already run through the most plausible faculty, so imagine my surprise when I bumped into Z of all people, who was desperate for a piss. Since there were no bathrooms on campus and I was already wet, I invited him under the footbridge, where he hosed me down like a burning building. "Nice work," Z said, zipping up. "I expect I'll see you at the big reading." "What does this have to do with poetry?" I asked, but Z was either hard of hearing or had learned not to notice such questions in advance. "You're going to be late," he said.

CRAZY JANE ADDRESSES CONGRESS

stop farting around with these shits. wash those messianic underpants and take this leak seriously. tis only your t'ird or your fart'. honor thy farter and mudder. urine: the army now? the soldiers are pissed and pooped. the solar anus blows hotter than the world will bear now that it's on its way out. say goodbye to your puckered uncle en route to planet plunket. i'm tired of taking this shit—it hurts! stop wiping me off the ass of the earth like i chose this remote commode. i'm not a squatter; i just live here, and i can't afford water so i only drink beer. i'm slightly dehydrated and my pupils are dilated 'cause i got annihilated sometime last night again. i got dishpan hands to prove i know the prune principle. coffee, figs, and cigarettes are all you ever gave me, o semi-colonic american government! otherwise it was cheese only readers could digest. now i'm flush with excitement. did you say i'm like your ace in the hole or invite me to lick your asshole? either way i refuse to serve. it's your duty, so clean it up; my behind schedule is full. coprophagia is overrated but it's not as bad as what you expect me to swallow. stop eating eggs at sammy's, evoking some boogie you can't achieve by means of leaden reference while i mob my oldschool sideways through the zoo of human experience. behold my mechanical animals.

rumor has it we're still alive though i'm positive we died on an is-
land surrounded by nuts we couldn't afford. this sweater was
made in the u.s.a. which is anywhere you close your eyes and pre-
tend there aren't any consequences. you've eaten our culture into
a corner. what's the difference between crack and nutrasweet?

ELEGIES

LIGHT SLEEPER (ELEGY FOR GEORGE HARRISON)

O! Who could glide noiselessly? **CAMILLO PESSANHA**

orange ganges! receive these grains:

i don't like nan i like cobra it sent me burning down the river
they combed the ghats for me but there were too many there
a quiet epitaph approached the circle circling
as the glob of globe begat the grid that girdles earth

i seek its internal gurgle
the plaid pajamas of a resort to form takes refuge in the river's
    sunken quilt
when the boat i never said i was on passes singing you'll know
my sweet defenestration

ANDRÉ BRETON'S APARTMENT

the madder runs
like blood

lifeblood of
the livebud

that kindles next to earth

the hair on the church is water
the lovebirds curve their crutches down

so long
to the sacred
palaces

so long to the fingerbone that lingers on

if i'm alive
it's no thanks to you

if i'm comatose
let's make the most of it

tomato ghost

rude twilight

ruby tear

discipline disappears
between the shapeless necklace
and the cloudy robe of shrapnel

in the absence
of incense

no balm can grease
the throbbing temples

of the rotting world

FOR THOM GUNN

i'm sorry you had to die at a time when evil's got this country by the balls, cracks them and sucks them like eggs. in a final rake of the heart throw out some vinyl records i can throw on like a pair of pants and dance my way through this crap. i'm so happy i'm suicidal, like a psilosybin trip that's moved in for good and his name is george bush, a hallucinogenic indole obtained from a fungus. fuck'm. it's a sad vacation; what can i say? i only write po-ems of death these days. *nightmare of beasthood, snorting, how to wake?*

MILDRED BEGLEY

is not an anthony trollope novel
& scans the same as *instant karma*
mildred begley's gonna get you

went to school with kerouac
better recognize aunt mildred
etc., in these artifacts:

mildred begley
                        born in lowell
in the year of *magnetic fields*

milltown owned
by utopian capitalists
—fascists that is—

family of amy & robert
& james russell lowell
the fucking assholes of poetry

mildred begley's gonna get you
the lyrics to *barney google*
& a book by andrew joron

she will say: what we say
about the poem is not the poem
we must always remember

the sky might open a bird
to read & head to death
without quite realizing it

without fear of meeting
on the road an unforeseen
memory to hinder the passage

between two verses. in the age
of digital media it's still
possible to lose a poem

through a series of miscalculations

"I HAVE SEEN ENOUGH"

for Nancy Peters

inside his apartment where he and i smoked the roach of his age and my youth for the first time since he died, examining his papers. as if on cue the toilet explodes. ("the plumbing is victorian," he'd say, apologetically, instructing a guest not to flush; only he had the right touch.) "i have seen enough," written on a page dated 7 years, 2 days before his death. the odor of the place clings to my clothes, the way it pervaded his books, a compound of tobacco and indefinable fragrances. for the rest of the day i attract birds: pigeons roost on my lap; a rooster runs by; a quartet of wild parrots buzz me mid-thigh at high speed. all this in downtown san francisco. surreality is real. even a sparrow nearly bumps into me. another sits next to me, contemplating me. she tells me a story. they were walking in a park when they saw two birds mating in the grass suddenly swallowed by a lawnmower, and here are the letters he wrote to the superintendent of parks, and the poems against the lawnmower. sometimes the pages seem effortless, stretching into passages exuberant and harrowing. there were years he didn't write, yet you'd never know seeing his papers arranged in decades. these are poet's ashes, volcanic and smoldering still. to lose this scent is to enter permanent exile.

ORPHEUS

sometimes i tell you to go to hell and when you're gone i regret sending you there. but getting you back isn't easy. i traverse a burnt plain to a remote antigrotto where the hall of mad lovers teeters precariously between boredom and satisfaction. as long as it doesn't tip we're good: "like heine in paris," as the fish say when they fall from the frying pan. the path is littered with mirrors i've broken, but the interior's unlike what you'd expect. one minute it sprawls like a suburb; next it's close as an elevator; finally it resolves into restaurants where shades of my former lovers gather to compare notes. you sit in the center at a table for two with the devil, who resembles me but has better manners and a lot more money. he listens sympathetically. "my brother is dead," you say. "the light of the world has gone out." "what does your husband do for a living?" he asks, and i can't but admire his deftness. i strike him til he shatters between my knuckles. i'm the one bleeding and the hole in the mirror laughs. "there's no returning from hell," it says. "there's only buying furniture."

FOUR TUNE

fuck
love

none
same

lame
name

rust
talk

tall
cans

lost
ball

mall
girl

dirt
mill

lime
pill

dime
toll

bell
pole

pale
pile

bile
lies

life
dies

diet
wise

duet
ties

blue
ones

coal
goal

lone
lust

tone
dust

bone
must

hone
thus

bore
pour

more
brie

lump
lore

rump
rope

hope
prop

dont
stop

folk
rock

suck
cock

milk
sock

silk
cunt

cant
rant

side
ways

fart
note

flat
hand

nose
song

king
kong

gone
yawn

yard
laws

over
bear

beer
pawn

luck
gone

lock
vent

peep
show

gold
gulp

face
once

butt
plug

fore
play

plan
five

what
wife

want
wont

stay
live

sick
nest

fast
dead

pain
made

help
less

horn
toot

lash
mate

coke
cost

poet
loss

slow
down

salt
slot

book
bent

open
nope

shut
that

shit
some

time
past

last
word

will
plow

loud
land

boom
bust

bomb
bats

felt
deft

weft
heft

gift
dick

with
kick

back
sack

gums
gems

cash
math

pure
sure

true
stew

iran
iraq

cuba
hugo

neon
yugo

pipe
line

weak
link

leak
week

melt
snow

huge
mess

fail
test

fake
safe

hush
bush

mush
tush

good
spot

evil
city

waif
look

took
more

fork
from

dork
dome

pork
wars

turf
goof

crap
cure

hell
hole

soil
soul

burn
long

kiss
neck

lift
rift

nice
pets

fits
mood

self
ebbs

when
sane

mind
ends

fist
feud

pick
path

part
lips

rain
drip

wets
feet

drop
sail

male
gaze

limp
duck

dull
doll

holy
moly

dank
tank

dark
tint

clay
hand

toss
moss

dung
heap

dunk
tent

bunk
beds

fall
guys

blow
hard

navy
bean

army

chow

jail

term

drug

hurt

sexy

type

text

here

dear

fool

lose

dumb

idea

fear

smug

past

know
fact

hate
late

amer
acts

snot
suit

puke
poem

keep
sake

NOTES AND ACKNOWLEDGMENTS

The epigraph by Camillo Pessanha to "Light Sleeper" is the Vekony translation. The title comes from a song on *The Box Car Sessions* (Warner Bros., 1994) by Saafir, the Saucee Nomad.

The epigraph by Philip Lamantia to "Inside the Coin" is from his essay "Radio Voices" (*Cultural Correspondence*, nos. 12–14, ed. Paul Buhle, 1981). The epigraph by Georges Bataille to *The Rogue Hague* is from *The Accursed Share, Volume 1* (Zone, 1991), translated by Robert Hurley.

Some of these poems appeared in the following magazines: *26, Fence, Kenning, The Hat, Mirage #4/Periodical, Untitled, Urvox, Verse, Yen Agat*; the anthology *Bay Poetics* (Faux Press, 2006); and in or on the following cds: *Rectangle, Un Nuco Sabe* (Stereorrific, 2003), *Various Artists, I'm With Cupid* (Waxfruit, 2004), *Surrealism's Bad Rap* (NarrowHouse Recordings, 2006).

The author extends his thanks to everyone involved in the above projects, and to Jeff Clark, Andrew Joron, and Eileen Tabios for making the present book possible.

Born in Lawrence, Massachusetts in 1972, Garrett Caples is a poet living in Oakland, California. He is the author of *The Garrett Caples Reader*, *er, um*, and *The Philistine's Guide to Hip Hop*. He's published numerous essays, articles, and reviews, and currently writes on hip hop for the *San Francisco Bay Guardian*.

SAN FRANCISCO & ST. HELENA

MERITAGE PRESS PROJECTS

[SINCE 2001]

"COLD WATER FLAT" (2001). Signed and numbered etching
by Archie Rand and John Yau. Limited edition of 37.

100 MORE JOKES FROM THE BOOK OF THE DEAD (2001). A monograph
documenting a collaboration by Archie Rand and John Yau.

ER, UM (2002). Poems by Garrett Caples and drawings by Hu Xin.
Limited edition of 75 copies. Signed and numbered by the poet.

MUSEUM OF ABSENCES (2003). Poems by Luis H. Francia.
(Copublished with the University of the Philippines Press.)

OPERA: POEMS 1981-2001 (2003) by Barry Schwabsky.

VEINS (2003). A poetry broadside by David Hess.

[WAYS] (2004). A poetry-art collaboration by Barry Schwabsky and
Hong Seung-Hye. (Copublished with Artsonje Center, Seoul.)

THE ORACULAR SONNETS (2004). An e-publication of a visual poetry
collaboration between Mark Young and Jukka-Pekka Kervinen.

*PINOY POETICS: A COLLECTION OF AUTOBIOGRAPHICAL AND CRITICAL ESSAYS
ON FILIPINO AND FILIPINO-AMERICAN POETICS* (2004). Edited by Nick Carbo.

THE OBEDIENT DOOR (2005). Poems by Sean Tumoana Finney
and drawings by Ward Schumaker.

THE FIRST HAY(NA)KU ANTHOLOGY (2005). Edited by Jean Vengua and
Mark Young. (Copublished with xPress(ed), Espoo, Finland.)

NOT EVEN DOGS (2006). Hay(na)ku Poems by Ernesto Priego.

UNPROTECTED TEXTS: SELECTED POEMS (1978-2006)
(2006). Poems by Tom Beckett.

DÉRIVE (2006). A poetry-art collaboration by Bruna Mori and Matthew Kinney.

KALI'S BLADE (2006). Poems, prose and collaborations by Michelle Bautista.

DAYS POEM, VOLUMES. 1 & 2 (2007) by Allen Bramhall.

FRAGILE REPLACEMENTS (2007). Poems by William Allegrezza.

COMPLICATIONS (2007). Poems by Garrett Caples.

PRAU (2007). Poems by Jean Vengua.